TAKE THE LEAD
PIANO

Musicals

Series Editor: Anna Joyce
Editorial, production and recording: Artemis Music Limited • Design and production: Space DPS Limited • Published 2001

IMP
International MUSIC Publications

Demonstration Backing

Fame
from *Fame*

Words by Dean Pitchford
Music by Michael Gore

Bright pop feel

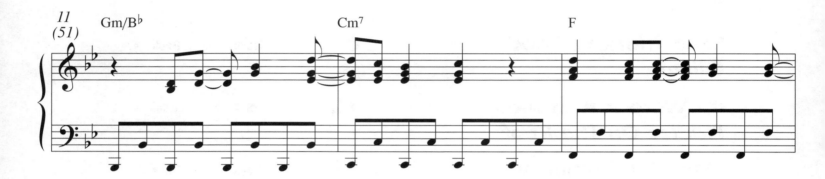

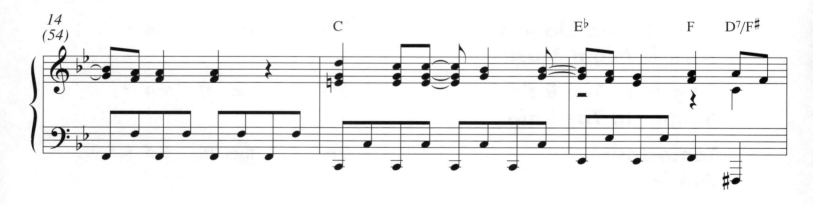

4

Demonstration Backing

Food Glorious Food
from *Oliver*

Words and Music by Lionel Bart

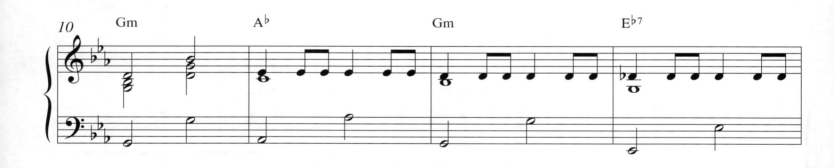

If I Were A Rich Man
from *Fiddler On The Roof*

Words by Sheldon Harnick
Music by Jerry Bock

Whatever your instrument is...
you can now

TAKE THE LEAD

- Each book comes with a professionally recorded CD containing full backing tracks for you to play along with, and demonstration tracks to help you learn the songs

- Ideal for solo or ensemble use - in each edition, songs are in the same concert pitch key

- Each book includes carefully selected and edited top line arrangements; chord symbols in concert pitch for use by piano or guitar

- Suitable for intermediate players

"A great way to get some relaxing playing done in between the serious stuff"
Sheet Music Magazine

Discover The Lead

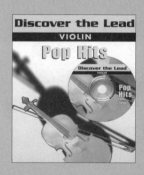

- This new 'spin off' of the Take The Lead series is ideal for beginners of all ages, grades 1-3

- The books contain simplified arrangements of well-known tunes to help the beginner develop reading and playing skills, while increasing confidence as a soloist

- Includes a useful fingering chart plus a CD with full backing and demonstration tracks

- Lots of helpful hints and technical tips to help you get to know your instrument

SHARE THE LEAD

- All pieces have been carefully selected and arranged at an easy level to provide fun material for today's instrumentalists

- All the arrangements work not only as duets for one particular instrument, but with all other instruments in the series (i.e. the flute book works with the clarinet book)

- The professionally recorded CD allows you to hear each song in 4 different ways – a complete demonstration of the track; part two plus backing so you can play along on part one; part one plus backing so you can play along on part two; and the backing only so you and a friend can Share The Lead!

A

Air That I Breathe, The	TTL	90s Hits
Air On A G String (Bach)	DTL	Classical Collection
All Through The Night	TTL	British Isles Folk Songs
Amazed	TTL	Ballads
Angels	TTL	90s Hits
Ave Maria (Schubert)	DTL	Classical Collection

B

Bailamos	TTL	Latin
Be-Bop-A-Lula	TTL	Rock 'n' Roll
Beautiful Stranger	STL	Film & TV Hits
Because You Loved Me	TTL	Movie Hits
Believe	TTL	Number One Hits
Birdland	TTL	Jazz
Blue Monday	TTL	Movie Hits
Blue Suede Shoes	TTL	Rock 'n' Roll
Blueberry Hill	TTL	Rock 'n' Roll

C

Careless Whisper	TTL	Number One Hits
Charlie's Angels	STL	Film & TV Hits
Chattanooga Choo Choo	TTL	Swing
Cherry Pink And Apple Blossom White	TTL	Latin
Choo Choo Ch'Boogie	TTL	Swing
C'mon Everybody	TTL	Rock 'n' Roll
Coronation Street	TTL	TV Themes
Christmas Song, The (Chestnuts Roasting On An Open Fire)	TTL	Christmas Songs

D

Dance Of The Sugar Plum... The Nutcracker (Tchaikovsky)	TTL	Classical Collection
Dancing Queen	TTL	Number One Hits
	STL	Chart Hits
Desafinado	TTL	Jazz
Don't Get Around Much Anymore	TTL	Jazz
Don't Say You Love Me	STL	Film & TV Hits
Don't Tell Me	DTL	Pop Hits

E

Everybody Needs Somebody To Love	TTL	The Blues Brothers
(Everything I Do) I Do It For You	TTL	Movie Hits

F

Fascinating Rhythm	TTL	Jazz
Flying Without Wings	TTL	Number One Hits
	STL	Chart Hits
Frosty The Snowman	TTL	Christmas Songs
Frozen	TTL	90s Hits

G

Genie In A Bottle	DTL	Pop Hits
Get Here	TTL	Ballads
Gimme Some Lovin'	TTL	The Blues Brothers
Great Balls Of Fire	TTL	Rock 'n' Roll
Green Door, The	TTL	Rock 'n' Roll
Greensleeves	TTL	British Isles Folk Songs
Guantanamera	TTL	Latin

H

Hall Of The Mountain King from Peer Gynt (Grieg)	TTL	Classical Collection
Have Yourself A Merry Little Christmas	TTL	Christmas Songs
Holler	DTL	Pop Hits
How Do I Live	TTL	90s Hits
	STL	Chart Hits

I

I Believe	STL	Film & TV Hits
I Don't Want To Miss A Thing	TTL	90s Hits
	TTL	Movie Hits
	TTL	Ballads
I Will Always Love You	TTL	Movie Hits
	TTL	Number One Hits
I'll Be There For You (Theme from Friends)	TTL	90s Hits
	TTL	TV Themes
	STL	Film & TV Hits
I've Got A Gal In Kalamazoo	TTL	Swing
In The Mood	TTL	Swing
It Don't Mean A Thing (If It Ain't Got That Swing)	TTL	Swing

J

Jailhouse Rock	TTL	Rock 'n' Roll
Jersey Bounce	TTL	Swing

L

La Bamba	TTL	Latin
La Donna E Mobile From Rigoletto (Verdi)	DTL	Classical Collection
La Isla Bonita	TTL	Latin
Largo From New World Symphony (Dvorak)	DTL	Classical Collection

L cont.

Leaving Of Liverpool, The	TTL	British Isles Folk Songs
Let's Twist Again	TTL	Rock 'n' Roll
Life Is A Rollercoaster	DTL	Pop Hits
Little Bit More, A	TTL	Ballads
Little Donkey	TTL	Christmas Songs
Livin' La Vida Loca	TTL	Number One Hits
	TTL	Latin
Loch Lomond	TTL	British Isles Folk Songs
Love's Got A Hold On My Heart	STL	Chart Hits
Lullaby From Wiegenlied (Brahms)	DTL	Classical Collection

M

Match Of The Day	TTL	TV Themes
(Meet) The Flintstones	TTL	TV Themes
Men Behaving Badly	TTL	TV Themes
Men Of Harlech	TTL	British Isles Folk Songs
Millennium	DTL	Pop Hits
Minnie The Moocher	TTL	The Blues Brothers
Misty	TTL	Jazz
More Than Words	STL	Chart Hits
Morning From Peer Gynt (Greig)	DTL	Classical Collection
My Funny Valentine	TTL	Jazz
My Heart Will Go On	TTL	90s Hits
	TTL	Ballads
	STL	Chart Hits

O

Ode To Joy From Symphony No. 9 (Beethoven)	DTL	Classical Collection
Old Landmark, The	TTL	The Blues Brothers
One O'Clock Jump	TTL	Jazz
Oye Mi Canto (Hear My Voice)	TTL	Latin

P

Peak Practice	TTL	TV Themes
Pennsylvania 6-5000	TTL	Swing
Polovtsian Dances from Prince Igor (Borodin)	TTL	Classical Collection
Pure Shores	STL	Film & TV Hits

R

Radetzky March (Strauss)	TTL	Classical Collection
Reach	DTL	Pop Hits
Rose, The	TTL	Ballads
Rudolph The Red-Nosed Reindeer	TTL	Christmas Songs

S

Santa Claus Is Comin' To Town	TTL	Christmas Songs
Say What You Want	DTL	Pop Hits
Scarborough Fair	TTL	British Isles Folk Songs
Searchin' My Soul	STL	Film & TV Hits
Seasons In The Sun	DTL	Pop Hits
Shake A Tail Feather	TTL	The Blues Brothers
She Caught The Katy And Left Me A Mule To Ride	TTL	The Blues Brothers
Sheep May Safely Graze (Bach)	TTL	Classical Collection
Simpsons, The	TTL	TV Themes
Skye Boat Song, The	TTL	British Isles Folk Songs
Sleigh Ride	TTL	Christmas Songs
Something About The Way You Look Tonight	STL	90s Hits
Soul Limbo	TTL	Latin
Spring From The Four Seasons (Vivaldi)	DTL	Classical Collection
Star Wars (Main Theme)	TTL	Movie Hits
String Of Pearls, A	TTL	Swing
Summertime	TTL	Jazz
Swan, The from Carnival of the Animals (Saint-Säens)	TTL	Classical Collection
Swear It Again	TTL	Ballads
Sweet Home Chicago	TTL	The Blues Brothers
Symphony No. 40 in G Minor, 1st Movement (Mozart)	TTL	Classical Collection

T

Think	TTL	The Blues Brothers
Toreador's Song, The from Carmen (Bizet)	TTL	Classical Collection

W

When Irish Eyes Are Smiling	TTL	British Isles Folk Songs
When You Say Nothing At All	TTL	Number One Hits
	STL	Chart Hits
	STL	Film & TV Hits
Wind Beneath My Wings, The	TTL	Movie Hits
	TTL	Ballads
Winter Wonderland	TTL	Christmas Songs

X

X-Files, The	TTL	TV Themes

Y

You Needed Me	TTL	Number One Hits
	STL	Chart Hits
You Can Leave Your Hat On	TTL	Movie Hits

Take The Lead

90s Hits
Air That I Breathe - I'll Be There For You - Something About The Way You Look Tonight - Frozen - How Do I Live - Angels - My Heart Will Go On - I Don't Want To Miss A Thing

Movie Hits
Because You Loved Me, Blue Monday, (Everything I Do) I Do It For You, I Don't Want To Miss A Thing, I Will Always Love You, Star Wars, The Wind Beneath My Wings

TV Themes
Coronation Street, I'll Be There For You (Theme from Friends), Match Of The Day, (Meet) The Flintstones, Men Behaving Badly, Peak Practice, The Simpsons, The X-Files

The Blues Brothers
She Caught The Katy And Left Me A Mule To Ride - Gimme Some Lovin' - Shake A Tail Feather - Everybody Needs Somebody To Love - The Old Landmark - Think - Minnie The Moocher - Sweet Home Chicago

Christmas Songs
Winter Wonderland - Little Donkey - Frosty The Snowman - Rudolph The Red Nosed Reindeer - Christmas Song (Chestnuts Roasting On An Open Fire) - Have Yourself A Merry Little Christmas - Santa Claus Is Comin' To Town - Sleigh Ride

Swing
Chattanooga Choo Choo - Choo Choo Ch'Boogie - I've Got A Gal In Kalamazoo - In The Mood - It Don't Mean A Thing (If It Ain't Got That Swing) - Jersey Bounce - Pennsylvania 6-5000 - A String Of Pearls

Jazz
Birdland - Desafinado - Don't Get Around Much Anymore - Fascinating Rhythm - Misty - My Funny Valentine - One O'Clock Jump - Summertime

Latin
Bailamos - Cherry Pink And Apple Blossom White - Desafinado - Guantanamera - La Bamba - La Isla Bonita - Oye Mi Canto (Hear My Voice) - Soul Limbo

Number One Hits
Believe, Cher - Careless Whisper, George Michael - Dancing Queen, Abba - Flying Without Wings, Westlife - I Will Always Love You, Whitney Houston - Livin' La Vida Loca, Ricky Martin - When You Say Nothing At All, Ronan Keating - You Needed Me, Boyzone

Classical Collection
Sheep May Safely Graze (Bach) - Symphony No. 40 in G Minor, 1st Movement (Mozart) - The Toreador's Song from Carmen (Bizet) - Hall Of The Mountain King from Peer Gynt (Grieg) - Radetzky March (Strauss) - Dance Of The Sugar Plum Fairy from The Nutcracker (Tchaikovsky) - Polovtsian Dances from Prince Igor (Borodin) - The Swan from Carnival of the Animals (Saint-Säens)

Rock 'n' Roll
Be-Bop-A-Lula - Blue Suede Shoes - Blueberry Hill - C'mon Everybody - Great Balls Of Fire - The Green Door - Jailhouse Rock - Let's Twist Again

Ballads
Amazed - Get Here - I Don't Want To Miss A Thing - A Little Bit More - My Heart Will Go On - The Rose - Swear It Again - The Wind Beneath My Wings

British Isles Folk Songs
All Through The Night - Greensleeves - The Leaving Of Liverpool - Loch Lomond - Men Of Harlech - Scarborough Fair - The Skye Boat Song - When Irish Eyes Are Smiling

Share The Lead

Chart Hits
Dancing Queen - Flying Without Wings - How Do I Live - Love's Got A Hold On My Heart - My Heart Will Go On - More Than Words - When You Say Nothing At All - You Needed Me

Film & TV Hits
Beautiful Stranger - Charlie's Angels - Don't Say You Love Me - I Believe - I'll Be There For You - Pure Shores - Searchin' My Soul - When You Say Nothing At All

Discover The Lead

Pop Hits
Don't Tell Me - Genie In A Bottle - Holler - Life Is A Rollercoaster - Millennium - Reach - Say What You Want - Seasons In The Sun

Classical Collection
Air On A G String (Bach) - Ave Maria (Schubert) - La Donna E Mobile from Rigoletto (Verdi) - Largo from New World Symphony (Dvorak) - Lullaby from Wiegenlied (Brahms) - Morning from Peer Gynt (Grieg) - Ode To Joy from Symphony No. 9 (Beethoven) - Spring from The Four Seasons (Vivaldi)

Whatever your instrument is... you can now

TAKE, DISCOVER & SHARE

Available for Violin

7240A	TTL Swing
7177A	TTL Jazz
7084A	TTL The Blues Brothers
7025A	TTL Christmas Songs
7006A	TTL TV Themes
6912A	TTL Movie Hits
6728A	TTL 90s Hits
7263A	TTL Latin
7313A	TTL Number One Hits
7508A	TTL Classical Collection
7715A	TTL Rock 'n' Roll
8487A	TTL Ballads
9068A	TTL British Isles Folk Songs
7287A	STL Chart Hits
8493A	STL Film & TV Hits
8856A	DTL Pop
9165A	DTL Classical Collection

Available for Trumpet

7083A	TTL The Blues Brothers
7239A	TTL Swing
7176A	TTL Jazz
7262A	TTL Latin
7312A	TTL Number One Hits
7503A	TTL Christmas Songs
7507A	TTL Classical Collection
7714A	TTL Rock 'n' Roll
8486A	TTL Ballads
9067A	TTL British Isles Folk Songs
8494A	STL Film & TV Hits
8855A	DTL Pop
9164A	DTL Classical Collection

Available for Flute

6725A	TTL 90s Hits
7079A	TTL The Blues Brothers
7235A	TTL Swing
7172A	TTL Jazz
7022A	TTL Christmas Songs
7003A	TTL TV Themes
6908A	TTL Movie Hits
7259A	TTL Latin
7310A	TTL Number One Hits
7504A	TTL Classical Collection
7710A	TTL Rock 'n' Roll
8482A	TTL Ballads
9063A	TTL British Isles Folk Songs
7284A	STL Chart Hits
8490A	STL Film & TV Hits
8851A	DTL Pop
9160A	DTL Classical Collection

Available for Tenor Saxophone

6911A	TTL Movie Hits
7238A	TTL Swing
7175A	TTL Jazz
7082A	TTL The Blues Brothers
7311A	TTL Number One Hits
7637A	TTL Christmas Songs
7713A	TTL Rock 'n' Roll
8485A	TTL Ballads
9066A	TTL British Isles Folk Songs
9163A	DTL Classical Collection
8854A	DTL Pop

Available for Clarinet

7173A	TTL Jazz
7236A	TTL Swing
7080A	TTL The Blues Brothers
7023A	TTL Christmas Songs
7004A	TTL TV Themes
6909A	TTL Movie Hits
6726A	TTL 90s Hits
7260A	TTL Latin
7309A	TTL Number One Hits
7505A	TTL Classical Collection
7711A	TTL Rock 'n' Roll
8483A	TTL Ballads
9064A	TTL British Isles Folk Songs
7285A	STL Chart Hits
8491A	STL Film & TV Hits
8852A	DTL Pop
9161A	DTL Classical Collection

Available for Alto Saxophone

7005A	TTL TV Themes
7237A	TTL Swing
7174A	TTL Jazz
7081A	TTL The Blues Brothers
7024A	TTL Christmas Songs
6910A	TTL Movie Hits
6727A	TTL 90s Hits
7261A	TTL Latin
7308A	TTL Number One Hits
7506A	TTL Classical Collection
7712A	TTL Rock 'n' Roll
8484A	TTL Ballads
9065A	TTL British Isles Folk Songs
7286A	STL Chart Hits
8492A	STL Film & TV Hits
8853A	DTL Pop
9162A	DTL Classical Collection

Available for Piano

7178A	TTL Jazz
7026A	TTL Christmas Songs
7364A	TTL Latin
7441A	TTL Number One Hits
7509A	TTL Classical Collection
7716A	TTL Rock 'n' Roll
8488A	TTL Ballads
9069A	TTL British Isles Folk Songs
8857A	DTL Pop
9166A	DTL Classical Collection

Available for Drums

7179A	TTL Jazz
7027A	TTL Christmas Songs

Over The Rainbow
from *The Wizard Of Oz*

Words by E Y Harburg
Music by Harold Arlen

Demonstration   Backing

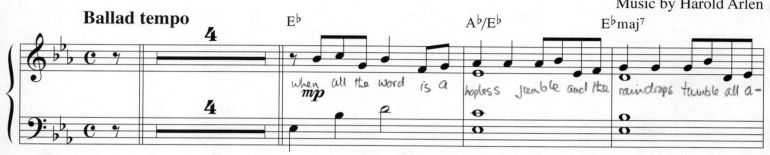

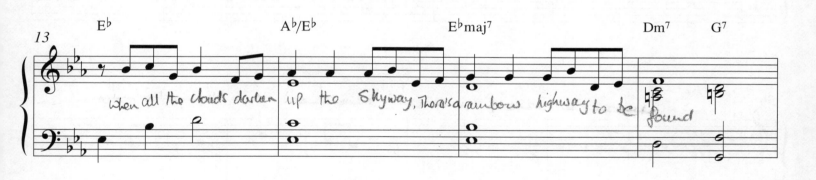

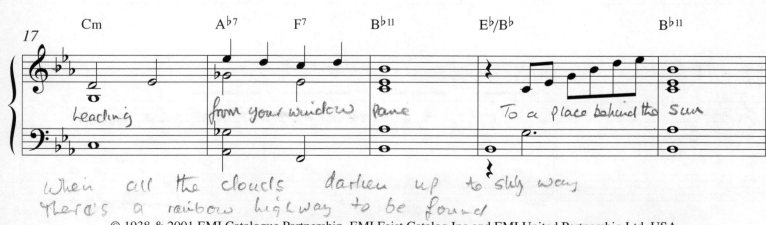

When all the clouds darken up to sky way
There's a rainbow highway to be found

leading from your window pane, To a place behind the sun

Demonstration   Backing

Singin' In The Rain
from *Singin' In The Rain*

Words by Arthur Freed
Music by Nacio Herb Brown

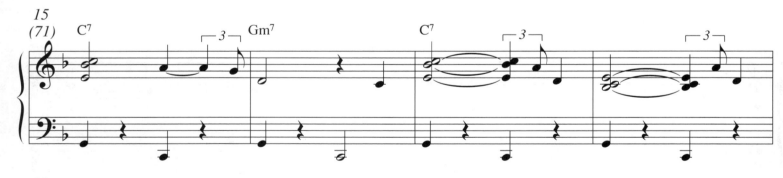

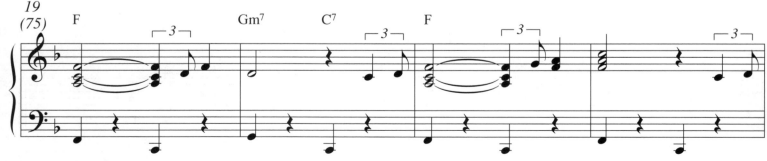

22

Demonstration   Backing

Send In The Clowns
from *A Little Night Music*

Words and Music by
Stephen Sondheim

Slowly

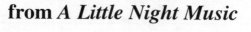

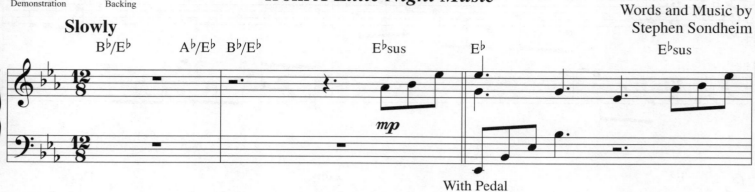

With Pedal

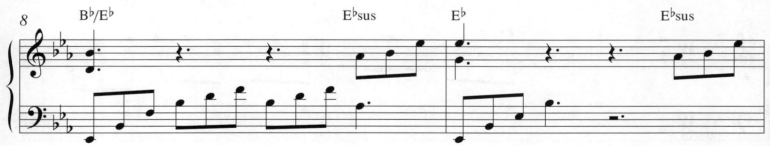

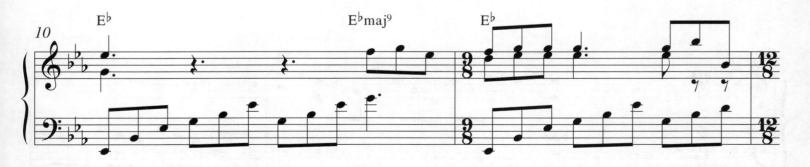

Tomorrow
from *Annie*

Words by Martin Charnin
Music by Charles Strouse

Demonstration   Backing

Wouldn't It Be Loverly
from *My Fair Lady*

Words by Alan Jay Lerner
Music by Frederick Loewe

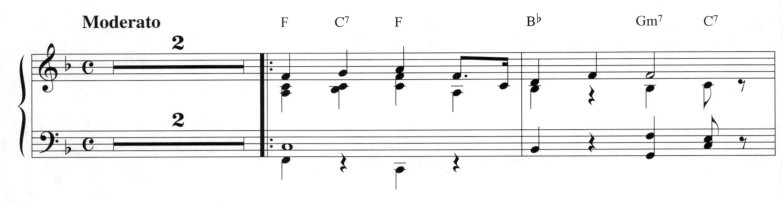

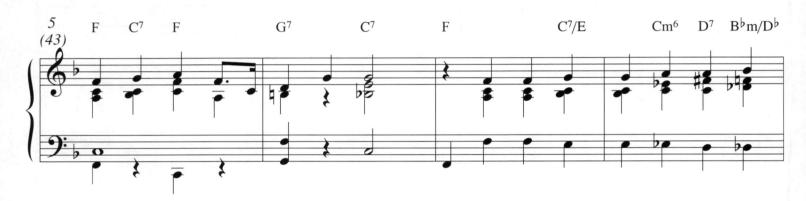

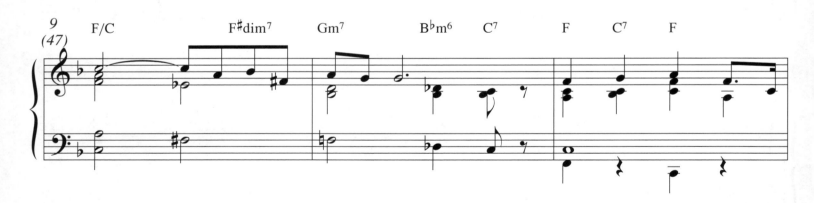

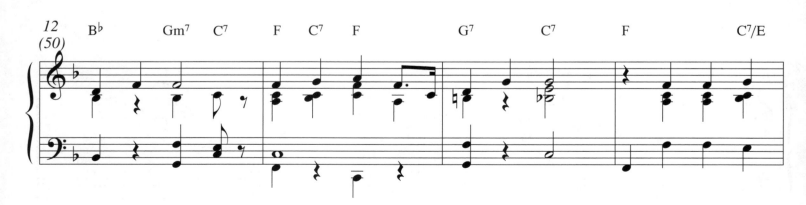

Printed by Halstan & Co. Ltd., Amersham, Bucks., England

TAKE THE LEAD

PIANO *on these classic musicals*

Fame
Fame

Food Glorious Food
Oliver

If I Were A Rich Man
Fiddler On The Roof

Over The Rainbow
The Wizard Of Oz

Send In The Clowns
A Little Night Music

Singin' In The Rain
Singin' In The Rain

Tomorrow
Annie

Wouldn't It Be Loverly
My Fair Lady

FEATURES

On The CD:

full backing tracks,
professionally arranged
and recorded

full demonstration recordings
to help you learn the songs

In The Book:

• carefully selected and edited
  piano arrangements

• chord symbols in concert pitch

Take The Lead is an integrated series for Alto Saxophone, Clarinet, Flute, Piano, Tenor Saxophone, Trumpet and Violin. In each edition all the songs are in the same concert pitch key, so the different instruments can play together.

All accompanying chord symbols are in concert pitch for use by piano or guitar.

IMP
International
MUSIC
Publications

ISBN 1-84328-028-0

9 781843 280286

ISMN: M57021 028 2

International Music Publications Limited
Griffin House 161 Hammersmith Road London W6 8BS England

Order ref: **9246A**

THE BEST OF

NAT KING COLE

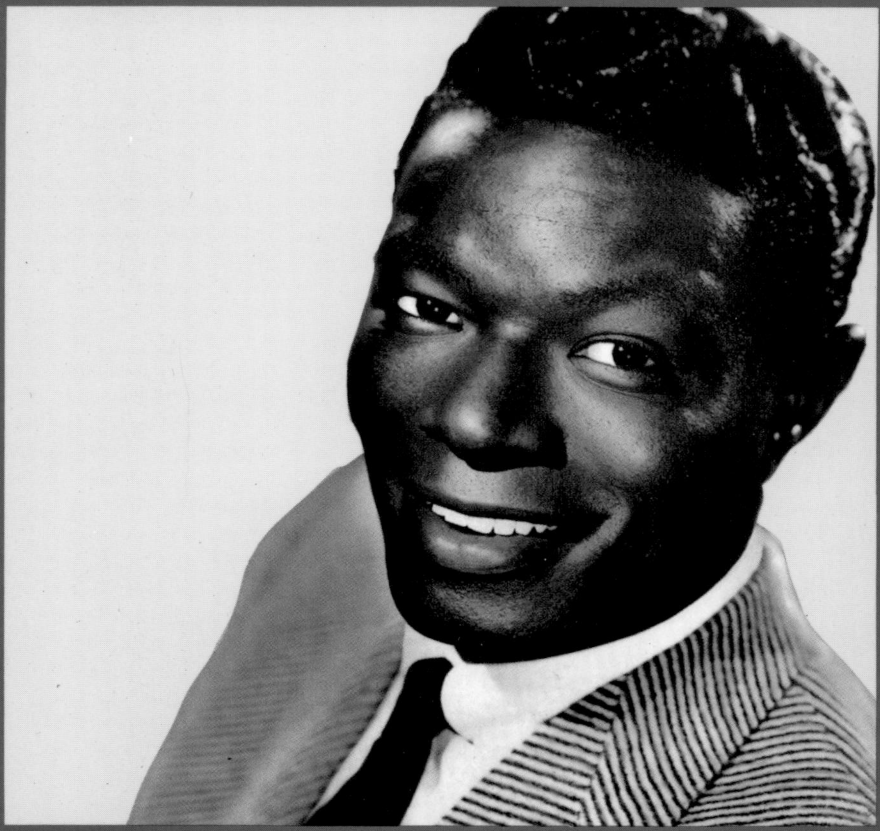